A Scream in the Vacuum
VOLUME 2

A Scream in the Vacuum
VOLUME 2

MATHAN SUBBIAH

RESOURCE *Publications* • Eugene, Oregon

A SCREAM IN THE VACUUM, VOLUME 2

Copyright © 2025 Mathan Subbiah. All rights reserved. Except for brief quotations in critical publications or reviews, no part of this book may be reproduced in any manner without prior written permission from the publisher. Write: Permissions, Wipf and Stock Publishers, 199 W. 8th Ave., Suite 3, Eugene, OR 97401.

Resource Publications
An Imprint of Wipf and Stock Publishers
199 W. 8th Ave., Suite 3
Eugene, OR 97401

www.wipfandstock.com

PAPERBACK ISBN: 979-8-3852-5343-2
HARDCOVER ISBN: 979-8-3852-5344-9
EBOOK ISBN: 979-8-3852-5345-6

VERSION NUMBER 070925

Dedication

Nothing has changed so nothing has been changed.

To the memory of my beloved parents, Helena and Subbiah, whose unwavering love and support laid the foundation for who I am today. To my brothers, Suthan and Sathan, and my sister, Honeyma, for always believing in me. And to my dear Subbiah Chithappa and Viji Chithi, who have been like second parents to me, thank you for your constant encouragement.

My journey hasn't always been easy. The symptoms started when I was 18, and at 25 I was diagnosed with bipolar disorder and schizophrenia. There have been dark times, moments when my illness manifested in violence. But through it all, the love and support of my family, especially my parents, gave me the strength to persevere. Their memory continues to inspire me.

This book is a testament to the strength of my family, and my own path towards healing.

Thank you for everything.

Nothing has changed so nothing has been changed.

This special dedication goes to:

Those cursed with mental illness, who suffer in silence, trapped in enduring pain, and facing endless misery without a hope of cure.

And to the countless who live in general suffering, caught in a cycle of pain and disappointment, enduring life's constant hardships.

To the oppressed, honest 98% who live in a skewed, rigged, and corrupt system, denied the light of a new dawn.

To those who are dying, persecuted, or living in constant fear of religious dogma, never allowed to lead the life they desire because of the shackles of religion and the poison and hatred spread by godmen and godwomen.

And most importantly to the innumerable innocents—children, fathers, mothers, and those who served in the tragedy called "line of duty"—who have lost their lives by mindless wars started by politicians, dictators, and in the name of religion.

Contents

Preface | *xiii*

Acknowledgments | *xv*

Introducing a New Resonance in Rhyming for My Poems: End-Letters Weave Rhyme | 1

Poems

Stranglehold | 5

Innocence | 7

The Smoke Tendrils of Life | 9

Justified Sex When in Marriage? | 11

Caste and Honor Killings | 13

Where It Was All Right and Where It All Went Wrong | 15

Adamant | 17

Casting Couch | 19

Ultimately It Is How You Lived | 21

High | 23

Private Tears or Tears in Private | 25

Prejudice or Plain Simple Blessed and Grateful for the Unknown | 27

A Long Story | 29

How Death Should Be After You Have Lived | 33

The Only Solution | 35

Realization Shall Set You Free | 37

Fuck You Money | 39

Two Weddings and a Funeral | 41

Mental Illness | 43

Bike | 45

Verses Without Explanation

Stages. The Amusement and Regret Loop | 47

Crystal Ball Gazing | 47

Not Able to Fill the Empty Spaces. A Mind Unfit for Idleness | 47

Ideology of Hatred in Democracy. Majority Rule or Majority Rage? | 48

They Do See You. Felt Not Said | 48

Omnipresent Caveat. Truths with Asterisks | 48

Stressed Mode and Relaxed Mode | 49

A Voiceless Self | 49

FAQs | 50

Do You Know What You Want? | 50

Yes, It Is Unfortunate | 50

One of the Many Many Alternatives | 50

What's Missing? Numbers Don't Wrinkle | 51

Importance of Idleness. The Forgotten Virtue of Doing Nothing | 51

What You Are When You Have Passed Away. The Vanishing Point | 51

Being Idle Above a Certain Age | 51

If You Care for Your Mind and Heart. Checkmate and Tears | 52

Mental Illness. The Fractured Deck | 52

Just Like That | 52

Please Lose Your Cool | 52

Matter of Concern | 53

Many Those Who Are Better | 53

Children of Lesser God. Running Without Legs, Seeing Without Eyes | 53

Mental Illness | 53

What Is More Important? | 54

The One Who Has Lost It All | 54

Color Blind. Nature's Divide, Humanity's Choice | 54

A FOSSianist Way of Life | 54

Never Learning from History. An Old Tale or a Stale Tale | 55

A Small Nudge | 55

Ing Dynasty | 55

Bending the Time | 56

Drying Up of the Well of Tears | 56

In Search of Relief | 56

Appear. Breathe Easy. Disappear. | 57

Bloated Senses | 57

Seepage (Irony and Sarcasm) | 57

FAQs | 57

Stress Reliever | 57

The Right Way | 58

Derivative Life | 58

So He Says and So She Says | 58

Nine-Pin Bowling | 58

Mistakes and Corrections | 59

Small Pleasures | 59

Theirs and Yours | 59

Face Value | 59

63.84% | 60

Soliloquy | 60

Ing Dynasty | 60

Ing Dynasty | 61

Appear. Breathe Easy. Disappear. | 61

Ing-Dynasty | 62

Mental Illness | 63

A Gentle Man | 63

Verses With Explanation

Stages. The Amusement and Regret Loop. | 65

Crystal Ball Gazing | 65

Not Able to Fill the Empty Spaces. A Mind Unfit for Idleness. | 66

Ideology of Hatred in Democracy. Majority Rule or Majority Rage? | 67

They Do See You. Felt Not Said. | 68

Omnipresent Caveat. Truths with Asterisks. | 68

Stressed Mode and Relaxed Mode | 69

A Voiceless Self | 70

FAQs. | 70

Do You Know What You Want? | 71

Yes, It Is Unfortunate. | 71

One of the Many, Many Alternatives | 72

What's Missing? Numbers Don't Wrinkle. | 73

Importance of Idleness. The Forgotten Virtue of Doing Nothing. | 73

What You Are When You Have Passed Away. The Vanishing Point. | 74

Being Idle Above a Certain Age | 74

If You Care for Your Mind and Heart. Checkmate and Tears. | 75

Mental Illness. The Fractured Deck. | 75

Just Like That | 76

Please Lose Your Cool | 77

Matter of Concern | 77

Many Those Who Are Better | 78

Mental Illness | 78

Mental Illness | 79

What Is More Important? | 79

The One Who Has Lost It All | 80

Color Blind. Nature's Divide, Humanity's Choice. | 80

A FOSSianist Way of Life | 81

Never Learning from History. An Old Tale or a Stale Tale. | 81

A Small Nudge | 82

Ing Dynasty | 83

Bending the Time | 84

Drying Up of the Well of Tears | 84

In Search of Relief | 85

Appear. Breathe Easy. Disappear. | 85

Bloated Senses | 86

Seepage | 87

FAQs | 87

Stress Reliever | 88

The Right Way | 88

Derivative Life | 89

So He Says and So She Says | 89
Nine-Pin Bowling | 90
Mistakes and Corrections | 91
Small Pleasures | 91
Theirs and Yours | 92
Face Value | 92
63.84% | 93
Soliloquy | 94
Ing Dynasty | 94
Ing Dynasty | 95
Appear. Breathe Easy. Disappear. | 96
Ing-Dynasty | 97
Mental Illness | 98
A Gentle Man | 99

Preface

The scream continues.

In Volume 1, I laid bare the turbulence of a mind shaped by decades of bipolar disorder and schizophrenia—my first cry into the vacuum. This second volume goes deeper. These are not just writings; they are reverberations from a life lived on the edge of perception, where reality fractures and reforms at will. The work remains unfiltered, raw, and untamed—an archive of hallucinations, heartache, rage, clarity, and a stubborn will to continue.

I have seen too much to write cleanly and felt too much to write gently. These poems and thoughts bear witness to a world that dehumanizes those who struggle silently, and celebrates illusions while silencing inconvenient truths. But beneath that lies resilience—not the heroic kind, but the quiet, everyday version: waking up, breathing, and choosing to write. Always, to write.

If Volume 1 was a raw wound, Volume 2 is the continuation of that open cry—widening, evolving, refusing to close. I am still writing, and I will keep publishing. These pages carry stories of betrayal, desire, the weight of family, the failure of systems, and the complicated peace that sometimes emerges—not from resolution, but from acceptance. My words are still a call, not for pity or comfort, but for understanding.

Read them as you will. Take what you need. Leave what you can't face. But know this: this too, is the scream. Still echoing. Still human.

Acknowledgments

Nothing has changed so nothing has been changed.

This book wouldn't exist without the unwavering support of some incredible people in my life. There were times when the journey felt overwhelming, and mental illness threatened to consume me. But thanks to these close friends and relatives, I found the strength to keep going.

Loud, ER, Bright, Raam, John, Govind, Gum, Ash—we met as eighteen-year-olds, and here we stand, weathered but unbreakable, at fifty-seven. You haven't just shaped me as a person; you've been my safety net, my cheerleaders, and, more importantly, my financial lifelines on numerous occasions. You are all more than friends, and the words "thank you" barely scratch the surface of what your love and support mean to me. Quite frankly, without you, I might not be alive here today.

Dr. Suresh, Hepsi, Piraboo, Alex, Lakshmi, GL, Mr. Deen, "Red Label" Raj, Jayaraj, Selva Anna, Rum-esh, Aho-bulb, Lorry, Duba, Sivakumar—you guys were all lifesavers.

To all the doctors who provided vital support during my mental health journey, especially Dr. Jayakumar Nehru, who has been a lifeline for over 15 years and continues to take care of me, my deepest thanks.

A special thanks to my managing editor, Matthew Wimer and his team. Your constant guidance, support, and immense flexibility were extremely helpful throughout this process. Your belief in this project is a dream come true.

Poems

Introducing a New Resonance in Rhyming for My Poems: End-Letters Weave Rhyme.

An Original Rhyme Scheme Invention

In all my poems I have written so far, I have a newly invented style of rhyme, the End-Letters Weave Rhyme.

In the following collection of poems, you will encounter a distinct approach to rhyme, one that I have cultivated to create subtle yet resonant connections between the lines. While many of the poems are structured in quatrains, the traditional patterns of full rhyme are often eschewed in favor of what I call the End-Letters Weave Rhyme.

This style focuses on the sonic harmony created by the shared final letters of the words at the end of each line within a quatrain. Rather than relying on the full vowel and consonant sounds of traditional rhyme, the End-Letters Weave Rhyme operates on the principle of partial sonic agreement, establishing echoes and undertones that weave through the stanza.

Specifically, this technique manifests in the following ways:

First and Fourth Line Match

The final two, three, or four letters of the last word of the first line will be the same as the final two, three, or four letters of the last word of the fourth line. This creates a foundational connection, anchoring the beginning and end of the stanza with a shared sonic signature.

Second and Fourth Line Match

The final two, three, or four letters of the last word of the second line will be the same as the final two, three, or four letters of the last word of the fourth line. This establishes a further link, drawing the second line into the sonic embrace of the concluding line.

Alternating Internal Pairing

The final two, three, or four letters of the last word of the first line will be the same as the final two, three, or four letters of the last word of the third line, and the final two, three, or four letters of the last word of the second line will be the same as the final two, three, or four letters of the last word of the fourth line.

This introduces a more interwoven and alternating pattern of sonic connection. It creates a sense of internal echoing within the stanza, where the first and third lines resonate with each other through their shared endings, and the second and fourth lines form their own distinct sonic pair. This can establish a more complex and layered musicality within the quatrain.

Third and Fourth Line Match

The final two, three, or four letters of the last word of the third line will be the same as the final two, three, or four letters of the last word of the fourth line. This reinforces the pattern, binding the central line of the quatrain to its final resolution through shared end-letter sounds.

First and Second Line Match & Third and Fourth Line Match

The last two, three, or four letters of the last word of the first line will be the same as the last two, three, or four letters of the last word of the second line, and the last two, three, or four letters of the last word of the third line will be the same as the last two, three, or four letters of the last word of the fourth line. This creates a distinct paired rhythm within the stanza, establishing a subtle sonic connection between the opening couplet and a parallel resonance in the closing couplet.

All Four Lines Match

In some instances, the final two, three, or four letters of the last word of all four lines within the quatrain will be the same. This creates an even more intense sonic unity, where each line resonates with the others through a shared phonetic ending.

A Similar Principle in Poems Structured in Six-line Stanzas (sestets)

While the preceding explanation primarily focuses on the application of the End-Letters Weave Rhyme within four-line stanzas (quatrains), a similar principle of subtle sonic connection through shared end-letters will also be employed in poems structured in six-line stanzas (sestets). Within the sestet, the intention remains to create a nuanced fabric of sound, linking lines through the echoing of their final two, three, or four letters.

This will introduce a more expansive canvas for these sonic relationships to unfold, potentially creating more intricate rhythmic patterns and a richer harmonic texture across the six lines. The effect will be a continuation of the subtle resonance found in the quatrains, but with the added dimension of a longer form, allowing for more complex interplay and a deeper sense of underlying musicality to emerge throughout the stanza.

Why I Use This Form

The intention behind the End-Letters Weave Rhyme is to create a layering of subtle sonic connections, offering a sense of cohesion and musicality without the sometimes predictable nature of full rhyme. It is a way to build resonance and thematic links through nuanced phonetic echoes, inviting the reader to listen for the underlying harmonies within the verse.

An Invitation to Readers

I invite you to explore the poems that follow with an ear attuned to these End-Letters Weave Rhyme, discovering the ways in which these subtle sonic threads contribute to the overall texture and meaning of each piece.

Poems

Stranglehold

From the ancient times it was not the kings or chieftains but the shamans, others brain maim,

Their power over ordinary people it keeps on swelling and drowned the kings too merciless and wild,

However strong the king was it is the fear of unknown that keeps drawing him to him,

So, for every occasion under his mercy, from consecration of temples to when to opt for a child.

When to sow seeds, when the tide will rise in the river, when to conquer other lands,

Blindly believed him, what can be judged of the shamans, all blatant lies,

Mostly they were devoid of human emotions and earthly things didn't matter, always threatened with their wands,

Can it be said was power drunk, think it is very much applicable, they were of different species.

But were pivotal in everything, nothing progresses without their secretive chanting,

That strong perverted chain carried through generations, they became priests, painted themselves red,

Imagination soared, limitless stories, anecdotes, and poison for everything,

Not to lose control, tightly held only within family, secrets shared.

The world and science have advanced in leaps and bounds, revealing things astonishing,

But there is no relenting in the stranglehold of the religious head,

Even minute protest or reasoning brought wrath, lynching, or beheading,

It is pathetic that quantum physics and idiots are on the same plane, accept only this or be dead.

Innocence

It was when he was sixteen that he noticed the mild, soft, tiny hairs on his forearms and his upper lips sprouting,

Without him knowing, the biological clock started ticking and his hormones were raging,

He was puzzled, did not know the reason why something was happening to him, emotions in his body were surging,

The adult supervision and fear of elders reined in his desires, but the feeling was not relenting.

What was happening to his body he did not know, but something was afoot he knew without knowing,

That's when the new neighbors moved in and there she was, petite, did not initially notice him,

There was an emotional upheaval when he saw her delicate body and her slim hips, skipping and hopping,

Within a week she not only noticed him but was besotted; she wanted to touch him and kiss his lips, her only aim.

From where what to do with one's body did they know, nobody knows, the best part is they don't have any regrets,

Is it the primeval instinct that draws a boy to a girl and where to touch them, somehow knowing,

That wall in their colony with a distinct curve prevented anyone's gaze, and it knew too many secrets,

That's where he took her when dusk was deepening and darkness was descending.

From where she knew, it was natural, she guided his fingers to her nub down under and kissed him deeply,

They knew that much, that they had to stimulate their parts and did not know what else to do, postpubescent,

That's puppy love, who could prevent them—their parents, their brothers or sisters—no, to say simply,

They truly don't know what further to do, this stimulation making them peak, they are so innocent.

The Smoke Tendrils of Life

Borrowed one cent that was the cost of a filter cigarette, this was something at that time, was fourteen or somewhere there about,

Had seen the hep crowd always walking with a cigarette dangling at the edge of lips and also talking,

Fascinated the way they sucked on it and let the smoke out of nostrils and make round O's while blowing it out,

Was only fourteen years old then, close friends who lent money cautioned this is addictive better stop attempting.

Father was a smoker, did not seem like an action that is wrong or anything to feel guilty,

There was the concept of pocket money but was so middle class that didn't receive any,

When the family was away taking the burnt butt in father's ashtray and smoked it wasn't a difficulty,

It didn't stop there, took a few and went to the alley with friends and shared those to many.

The world explodes in bright colors and the heart is filled with great power,

Felt and actually acted as if the world is under the pair of feet, such confidence head high and trot,

Eighteen it was college and why is it so strange mostly smokers became friends, non-smokers very fewer,

It was also that age where smoking was something manly and talked about a lot.

From few went to twenty, twenty-five per day, the youth was gone was in late fifties,

Twist of fate or deeds of an ill mind, family was gone and living alone in darkened room and continuously brood,

The only company is one cigarette after another, as the smoke tendrils drifts so do good old memories,

Wracked with cough as if the lungs would burst out of mouth, somehow agony feels good.

Justified Sex When in Marriage?

There was this silent and shy guy who minded his own business, led a simple life on his own, no wrongdoings,

There were no high hopes, no ambition, no reaching to the top, just an average life,

But there were plenty of emotions, mostly loving and caring for family and siblings,

Especially fond of the only younger sister, wanted to give her a lovely life, was sure for someone she will be a good wife.

In the meanwhile, there was a cataclysm happening in office in the adjacent seat,

There was this amazing and beautiful girl, however simple he may be, was attracted, surprisingly unafraid,

It wasn't initiated by him, she was enamored by him, proposed, he was overjoyed, in a heartbeat,

He settled his little sister in a good family and then married this fascinating mermaid.

When going on bike met with accident, lost his manhood, it was irreversible, yes, it is the fate, it is inconsiderate,

The mermaid was loyal for a year, two years, three years, sex-deprived, broke in debacle,

Her heart was all loyal to him, but her body went mad, she couldn't tolerate,

There was another handsome guy, all considerate, in the next cubicle.

Couldn't resist the advances, he too wasn't of exploiting type, just another guy, plain,

Called her home, she went, little bit of wine and nice music, this guy knew cooking, all life long,

Sat at the table, first avoided eyes, then went bold, kissed deeply, again and again,

Years of longing for sex was satisfied, this is sex when in marriage, is it wrong?

Caste and Honor Killings

Man is capable of creating wonderful things when set mind to it, all wonderful, but despicable is patriarchy,

Equally capable of creating something that shows depravity, deviant purposely,

So created caste system, it is an inherent behavior in animals to form social hierarchy,

It affected all, benefitted a few, tore fabrics of society into shredded pieces mercilessly.

As years go by, by thousands of years, things should improve, this proved contrary,

It is only getting stronger, poison and sewerage-filled minds don't let it go, held them tight,

Falling in love is a natural thing, it is a powerful feeling, entire heart pleasant and extraordinary,

It doesn't discriminate, she met the untouchable low caste, and it was love at first sight.

Youth dares, doesn't think about consequences, times have changed so thought, were also in right age,

But so deep-rooted, intertwined with honor, objection started to take deadly form,

Death threats, eloped to somewhere far away, his principle was no sex before marriage,

Wedding over, with great love bride entered the decorated room with a glass of milk, as was norm.

The door came crashing down, and in went father and brothers of bride with sickles, from every pore bloodlust pour, sheer terror,

Dragged, thrashed the screaming, wailing bride outside, made her see everything, she too was almost dead,

Some things should never ever happen, this killing is one of them, and it is just bloodthirsty honor,

Held head by hair, bent it backwards, exposed throat, sawed and severed his head.

Where It Was All Right and Where It All Went Wrong

With very small or even to say with no expectations at all, grew up middle class,

Did not know what is world or had any desire to know about what is world, no beyond means consumption,

Father, mother, brothers, sisters were cast in the same mold, simple people, heart transparent as glass,

If purchased a box of chocolates, that month is complete and filled with satisfaction.

There was no dearth of intelligence, inbuilt above average, a god's gift or parents' genes,

Breezed through education challenges, things to learn academically with ease and flair,

It is universal when things take a turn and become aware of self and desires, felt it in bones,

Even then did not dream big, maybe can say taking things as they came, just accepted, OK a little bit debonair.

Then came teenage, accompanied with surging and raging hormones, became quite a handful,

Natural attraction towards opposite sex became prominent, all-encompassing,

Wasn't anything attractive, there were others boys who were cute and more beautiful,

That's when seeds of disappointment were sowed, didn't find anyone to satisfy the urge that was pressing.

Exploits of others could hear constant, on more than one occasion saw it with own eyes, everywhere,

Still, it was a budding phase, so the emotions weren't that strong to cause permanent scar, no help from heavenly savior,

Is it so? Who knew about subconscious and who knew what was getting etched there,

Who knew what would be the repercussions, who knew how it would affect future behavior.

Not only physical aspects of humans are constantly evolving, so does the brain,

Along with evolution of brain, evolution of emotions couldn't prevent from happening,

So, it is natural that what would be categorized as negative emotions too intertwined, like wind and rain,

But why the term negative? Isn't it all part of one package, one self, one being, elation and suffering.

Adamant

This is the life, you are experiencing it right now, there is no yesterday or tomorrow,

Who has realized it? Tread cautiously, there aren't many but a few, fear of stigmatization,

Why should there be religion, why should there be a promise of afterlife, inbuilt sorrow,

Yet billions succumb to it, can't they realize it is all false and somebody's imagination.

But the very same billions get peace and meaning of life when they blindly follow,

The tale that is at least two thousand years old, and some faiths put the age to age of universe itself,

Not a nonsense, it is a matter of faith, and the majority will lynch you if you deny and disallow,

Can you give them the peace and tranquil that faith gives them? No, you cannot, excuse yourself.

When you think about it, so whose business is it? Definitely it is none of your business,

Cannot offer them peace, very well, what they believe is absolutely absurd and embarrassing,

What you got to offer as an alternative? Rationale, logic, and common sense, practicableness?

It won't work because they are mesmerized beyond your limit of rational understanding.

So, take the route that they have taken, that is, pray for them to get out of stupidity,

It won't work, in fact they will hoist a case of blasphemy and kill you, want to challenge?

Open the newspaper or read books in library, history repeats, religion kills, and it is real absurdity,

Eat ice cream and watch a movie with popcorn with your girlfriend, nothing is going to change.

Casting Couch

She was a bubbly girl born in a military family, no dearth of courage and boldness,

She cannot be termed as photogenic, this one is a real beauty as far as nature can push,

She was so beautiful, when thought deeply seems like God took a million years to perfect this goddess,

She was created and never walked but hopped and skipped in life and always in eager rush.

The craze was to do engineering, architecture, or become a dentist or doctor,

Didn't occur to take those paths, a natural in the art form of dancing and acting,

So, headstrong, whipped away societal pressure, pursued the path of heart, wanted to become an actor,

Was the center of attraction in any wedding and any occasion, so gaily and gracefully danced, coyly pouting.

The wedding video caught the attention of a famous but immoral director of films,

So, butter-smooth with years of experience with young girls, invited for discussion, lust for young steeped in gene,

Headstrong maybe, but innocent in worldly ways, went to the seven-star hotel, without qualms,

In bathrobe showing pubic hair, gave a scrap of paper filled with nonsense, asked her to enact the scene.

So, innocent, she gave her heart and soul, if judged without prejudice, an award-winning performance,

He described an intimate scene and asked her to shed her clothes to her inner wear, thought she is a pushover,

Puzzled at first, then caught on, disgusted, refused, then came physical force, a sexual advance,

All the dreams of a young, beautiful, innocent girl were devastated, ran out of the room, withdrew from world forever.

Ultimately It Is How You Lived

It was a crowded rave party, was compulsorily called, was into it, the spirit was such, the initial reluctance started fading,

Drinks flowed, girls kissed girls, guys kissed guys, touched tongue with that LSD stamp, the club filled with much on high youth,

She was gorgeous, caught the eye, came near swinging her sexy hips and lips pouting,

Pressed her body chest to chest, crotch to crotch, had ecstasy on her devilish but delicious mouth.

Crushed it on his lips, in the spirit of the party took it, by the time reached room,

She was wasted, it wasn't new, had been to plenty of such party, breathed out a sigh, barely managing own sway,

Laid her gently on the bed and tucked her tenderly underneath the bedsheet, inside mind colorful flowers bloom,

Brushed his lips on hers, few moments of yearning, but it quickly passed away.

More than slightly high, took the rum and cola on ice to a secluded balcony,

Was enjoying the twinkling diamond necklace of lights of the city, when heard the rustle of dress,

Turned, couldn't control the gasp, he hadn't seen such a beauty in his lifetime, broke away from party monotony,

Enjoying time alone, I hope I am not intruding, she said, voice honey and more husky, a real seductress.

For the first time in flinging years was speechless, she came close, the fragrance of her body intoxicating,

Silently stood for more than an hour, the fingers clasped each other, then did it right on the floor, slip and slide,

Raised her dress above hips, she groped feverishly for his hardness, pure bliss lasted overwhelming,

Exchanged numbers, many dates later, wore the wedding gown, ended with you may now kiss the bride.

High

When started the bike, engaged gear and moved, should it be shocking or surprised, this experience was not foreseen,
The handlebar of the bike has disappeared, there comes an invisible connection,
Between gestures of hands, the bike turns left or right, seems like only air is in between,
The top end of front suspension and mentally commanded the turning of bike, a wondrous alternative action.

Is that so? Or the liquid consumed or the substance that has been smoked, all actions languid,
Or both? The streetlights throw light, and it is like physical substance,
The asphalt turns into a jelly of molten tar, the wheels travel on that liquid,
There becomes a distinct separation between the lower body and the upper in this particular circumstance.

Each part of body functioning autonomously, who or what presses the clutch or front brake,
Who or what shifts the gear and, as in dream, operates the right leg brake, maybe the meaning of body reverb,
Never into hard stuff, already in many parts of world it is sanctioned and made legal, it is not anymore, a legal mistake,
Scientifically proven of its medicinal value, have to realize that it is a nature-given herb.

Manmade chemical concoction is good too, for it strips down and throws away inhibition, life slows down to a slow pace,

It is nonstop talking and giggling or nonstop laughing and giggling, from heart escapes a pleasant sigh,

When started and when reached the destination, it seems like had a long travel through space,

It all costs a few tens of dollars, no bliss can replace it, mother, did it need to be so high.

Private Tears or Tears in Private

In the first place there should not be any countries, continents, or states,

These are all bound by imaginary lines, what is the use? Absolutely useless,

Why is it that nobody learns lessons from history? Isn't it a simple thing? Everyone is earth's inmates,

It just takes a few hours in a day, maybe for a few weeks to understand it, for an intelligent mind even less.

Those imaginary lines have always been shifting throughout human history,

There have always been thousands of countries defined by those imaginary lines by someone's whims,

As usual, whenever a single person's or a small group of men's greed for territory,

That the innocent living humans who can feel pain and suffering are the victims.

The ancient Greeks, long back in the fifth century before Christ was born, the concept,

It was called democracy, but dig deeper, it goes even back to several centuries, a true principle,

The seeds of primitive democracy were sown, but why does it always have to be the rich to be elevated to that noble precept,

Who take over the important posts and ruin the concept of for the people and by the people.

When humanity has taken giant steps in technology, rational thoughts, and logic,

Should it be laughable or an occasion to lament that monarchy still exists, a perverse vanity,

Who cares for simple people? Who understands the suffering of a common man? Tragic,

Take the oldest democracy and the largest democracy, there is no relief for pathetic humanity.

Prejudice or Plain Simple Blessed and Grateful for the Unknown

It Is Better if It Is Just Called the Unknown

Am plain, simply abundantly blessed or plain, simple abundantly cursed, didn't actually sit for it and calculate,

The wise repeatedly say look at the bright side, count your blessings, and stay positive,

That is what determined to follow, something has to be tried hard to inculcate,

The deeply embedded thin thread was from birth, it was always happiness and joy, life's main motive.

Don't concentrate on the destination, enjoy the journey were added, true to a great extent,

That's what had always done, nobody taught, it was inbuilt, always rolled on floor laughing,

There was no need for stimulus to do that, from where this trait trapped inside mind, in constant state of excitement,

Did not know, but later in life realized this is what blessing is defined as, a rare thing already inbuilt deep within conscious being.

It is a constant battle between blessings and curses, couldn't these be more defined,

Just when realized what a blessed life it is, the curse smothers breath with a heavy pillow,

Gasp, the mortal fear taking hold of self, that small thread of blessing gains strength inside mind, deeply enshrined,

Slashing and tearing that smothering pillow, once again raise the head above insanity slow.

Many years pass in life, wonder why is it happening, blessed in particular, no answer,

This is what blessing is called as, did not know from where or by whom these holy seeds were sown,

Understanding and realizing that this is what is needed, not deeply going to the source of that power,

Forever in life being grateful that blessings surpass curses, forever indebted, let it just simply called the unknown.

A Long Story

By ages thirteen or fourteen a male will have a more obvious interest in sex than girls do,

Crush is a beautiful thing at that age, seems like she is the world, it is all consuming,

It happened, couldn't concentrate on anything, going out of the way to be with her, that bliss and yearning couldn't undo,

Dad got transferred to another place, and just as it started, she vanished from mind into nothing.

By ages of early twenties things became more real, there was another one, all-consuming again,

It was more sexual, it became hard to distinguish between what is love and what is lust,

Then there was more than one, many, youth took over and had sex with all of them, no guilt, that was certain,

It also had to do with some principles, no marriage before turning twenty-eight years past.

The so-called to settle in life was decided to that age, either arranged marriage or falling in love,

There is the inevitability of the office romance, because it involves the core essentials of that emotional thing,

Intimacy and familiarity, in this case familiarity doesn't breed contempt, fell for colleague, was as delicate as a dove,

After spending many intimate moments and conversations, tied the knot in a typical big fat wedding.

Hereditary aspects of health descended, and what the father had was passed on to the son, intensity crescendo,

In genes it is programmed, whatever efforts taken, a healthy lifestyle didn't prevent it from happening,

Trusted in modern medicines, in a few years the side effects started taking a toll on libido,

In marriage, making love at desired intervals is vital, dreaded erectile dysfunction took over, ruining everything.

She, on the other hand, had a healthy mind and body, very active, wanted sex, it is a basic need, became all consuming,

Love with one another can only handle the situation so long, the inevitable happened,

But she could have chosen anyone in the world, but her choice for a partner was devastating,

Was it betrayal from his best friend, or factors of intimacy and familiarity played again, felt conned.

Couldn't she have been more sensitive, it wasn't, she left with his best friend to make merry,

The whole world came crashing down, became bitter and disillusioned, and is he a traitor?

His own bodily disappointment didn't devastate the mind, it was the sheer treachery,

When kept on the plates of a fair scale, ultimately the blame couldn't be placed on any one factor.

Didn't believe in superstitions, didn't believe in false morals, didn't believe in fate, no pretenses,

Of not having sex before marriage, it was open, believed that the past acts didn't matter, until becoming married couples,

For a male or a female, there are so many things involved, hormones and circumstances,

But now started questioning, why had stuck with some kind of stupid principles.

What happened was problem with body and its parts, but it didn't affect any other quality,

The sheer brilliance and intelligence of mind, so immersed completely in work, pouring out sorrows but discreet,

Any sustained efforts will yield disproportionate returns, it was double so with mental ability,

In short years accumulated billions of dollars with little effort, and now world was under his feet.

Through these years medical science advanced in astonishing pace, and found remedy,

For all physical ailments, all side effects reduced almost completely, infused with new vigor,

Libido returned and erectile dysfunction vanished, was back to peak abilities of youth to satisfy bodily needs, was once again ready,

But didn't gloat, instead revised many of other previously held other principles and mental behavior.

Trashed the concept of love, made for each other, one man one wife for life,

Understood life much better, never turned cynical, that was always an anathema,

The one thing that was always believed and held as most important aspect in the period of strife,

Believe in sensory perceptions, why believe in imaginary things called God or soul or dogma.

Humans are divided into four major races, Caucasian, Mongoloid, Negroid, and Australoid,

With billions of girls and women in existence, they were easy to find, other way around they found him even otherwise,

With billions in hand, tasted many girls and women of the four major races, for sex paid,

There are one hundred and ninety-five countries, went further with tasting every one country wise.

But with one strict principle, never ever touched underage girls, always checked legal age,

Now running into late seventies, never relenting in vigor, living every straight man's dream, took life steady and slow,

So traumatizing was events of youth, never settled with any other one single woman, despised marriage,

It was all fun and party, but occasionally when sat alone by sunset, the heart did remain empty and hollow.

How Death Should Be After You Have Lived

- Doctors nowadays are a strange species, whatever tastes good for consumption is prohibited,

How can anyone resist potato chips, burgers, pizzas, Hyderabad mutton biryani, and ice cream,

Their heartbeats soar when patients tell them that they had alcohol and cashew nuts roasted,

Choke in their throat when patient tells them that they had five bull's-eyes' toasts and buttercream.

Started smoking when eighteen years old, though cautioned, did not know the power of its addictiveness,

Was in early stages of consuming alcohol regularly, since money was a problem, went for cheap stuff,

It came naturally, kept that habit once in a week, but the quantity was so much that made it a point to pass out into unconsciousness,

Born happy, lived happy, and made others happy too, every occasion of enhancement of pleasure later joined for every puff.

Is this what the common saying is, built like bull, it was applicable, could outdrink everyone under the table, just sometimes behaved like a barbarian,

The number of pegs didn't matter, it was starting at sunset and going on till sunrise,

Ate equally well, jokingly said vegetarian will kill, so feasted on fine dishes of nonvegetarian,

Youth to fifty tossed the earth around would be an understatement, sex too was regular, but never committed, very wise.

Now puff and pant when walked even a few meters, could not manage to climb a flight of stairs as if walking on slush,

Is it necessary to look back and regret? Think not, for every moment was filled with happiness and joy, all through life's path,

Whirled like a tornado when going anywhere, every day was filled with a gush of rush,

So, if the life has been fully lived, there won't be any regrets, only a small wish, a quick and sudden death.

The Only Solution

Was extremely attached to mother, father was a mason, she carried bricks on her head, countless years' skill,

Home was only as big as a king-sized bed, corrugated asbestos, soon she developed breathing problems, started ordinary,

Daily saw her wheeze and whole chest heave for tiny breath to inhale, went to work still,

Just to get him educated, was intelligent, soon discovered by the nun in the missionary.

The final day of her life arrived, begged for ambulance, the driver asked for bribe, nobody to condone,

Was barely managing for a single square meal, empty pockets, mother choked without air, had all along lived only in slums,

Died in the entrance of house, stared vacant for many days, when tears dried, heart turned into stone,

The whole system was corrupted from bottom to top, the money flowed to the top in unimaginable sums.

Committed the first murder of local councilor, there were millions hidden underneath the mattress at seams bursting,

Then systematically started murdering, extended area to corporates and politicians,

Knew that capitalism means create poverty, provide charity, was merciless in torturing before killing,

The corporates pressurized politicians, the politicians poured their fury on the police, who always behaved like barbarians.

However hard tried, he was too intelligent to leave any clue and vanished even before the blood dried, leaving back a scene gory,

It was already looted wealth from innocent and hardworking citizens, the politicians diverted stealthily,

Money from banks to corporates, their hidden wealth was more than equal to the GDP of that country,

Created a parallel system, soon petitions from citizens reached him, and gory murders only started increasing exponentially.

Realization Shall Set You Free

Only Little People Belittle

How many people have truly realized that this life on earth is only once,

Stay positive, don't accept straight away, say, hey, don't want negativity, just want to live,

A false premise to live, if born on this earth, there is equal measure of song and dance,

Positive and negative that will assault you, don't be blind, that is false positive.

See, it all begins with emotions in genes and DNA that has been programmed, for every livable moment,

That means when you are born a human, you are already stuffed with all kinds of emotions anyway,

Understand this, and you will not go to godmen or follow a religion to assuage all of torment,

Of emotions, because it is inside you, and you cannot just like that shed that away.

A snake may shed its skin, but these cannot be willed away, inbuilt emotions,

At least a hundred of thousands of years ago, from basic emotions, humans developed, sometimes makes self uneasy,

Much more complicated emotions, there is nothing you can do about it, left with no options,

You have to live with it, yes, it is difficult, and all you want is happiness, joy, and ecstasy.

Imagine the multibillion-dollar industry and the evil minds who try to exploit this state of being,

Your inability to at least lessen the impact of restlessness and feeling of misery and depression to even slightest degree,

The person who has understood it and accepted it is blessed, it needs a little bit of thinking,

When could choose what emotions needed and what is not wanted, realization shall set you free.

Fuck You Money

Chests puffed like helium-filled blimps, heads expanding like hot air balloons,

A spring in the step, best tailors fit the clothes, could meet everyone in their eyes,

Shoes shined like mirrors, made of exotic leather, handmade, only exclusive saloons,

Never carried a wallet in life, neither cards nor anything so inferior, recognizable anywhere? Yes.

The society where lived demanded in life and for the society a wife with a body fit for bikinis,

It is hard to comment about the beyond-words beautiful bride, proceeded to wed,

However ordinary a look has, it can be transformed into the looks of Adonis,

Spent the GDP of a small nation, they tied their nuptial knot, oh, all traditions followed.

Two days after, the habit returned, took the jet with plenty of coke and pretty girls' bodies with absolutely no flaw,

That is a given, it is inevitable that everyone likes to follow DiCaprio law, sexual mindset,

Not one, not two, at least a dozen, everyone aged below twenty-five, that is the law,

That's when can witness cat fights, many girls barely of legal age wanted a seat in the jet.

Prostrate on feet of elders, custom dictated, debauchery, wine, women, and drugs, easily can purchase,

Easily switched roles from devout to satisfying every carnal desire, a wild life journey,

No law, no court, no media can touch, leave alone implicate in a criminal case,

How many laws broke, cannot keep account, that's the power of fuck-you money.

Two Weddings and a Funeral

Her body was made of highly inflammable material, just holding hands ignited, became wet,

A massive fire erupted from within and joined the stream between legs,

Instant evaporation of ice in her heart and body, just when lips met,

Of all the promises, I love you is the purest, he said, but it was love, sex, and bye-bye and drugs.

He was an emotional type, easily the heart gets clawed and scratched, always ending up in tears,

His love was pure, she was mean by nature, broke and took away pieces of heart, couldn't erase that hurt stain,

Swore never again will look at a girl, it went on for several years,

Sisters are so intuitive to their brother's heart, they too suffered the pain.

It was a grand wedding, she too was in attendance, held a glass of wine in hand, well clear of dance floor gyrations,

He was frustrated of constant din, wine in hand, moved away to balcony, in silence to brood,

It didn't miss his sister's eye, the occasion when their eyes met and was momentarily flooded with emotions,

Skillfully guided brother to another balcony where she stood.

Opening sentences from both were, I will never ever get into a committed relationship,

Two weddings passed, it was same, then came the funeral, her heart cracked, poured everything out, the voice went whispering feeble,

That familiar pain and pleasure of heart tug reverberated powerfully between them, felt calmness descending like in a place of worship,

A thousand years passed, they were buried one on top of other, in death too inseparable.

* Four Weddings and a Funeral is a 1994 British romantic comedy film directed by Mike Newell. Lovely movie. If you get a chance watch it. The poem has the same theme. Love. I liked the title.

Mental Illness

Total solar eclipses occur somewhere on Earth every eighteen months on average, they say,

A lunar eclipse occurs approximately every six months, causing the moon to darken, nature's architecture,

But there is an insanity eclipse inside the head that occurs every minute, every hour, every day,

The darkness can be managed, but what about losing sanity, and it is every minute torture.

However hard tried, however hard trying to explain, it is not understood even by close loved ones, near and dear,

For at one moment appear normal, and the next moment agony and distortion of reality descends,

A scream and wail can be heard, but what when it happens inside head where no one can hear,

Appearing to be perfectly normal, it is a constant question from others, what's wrong, including close friends.

As time goes on watching this and hearing this constantly, the conclusion by others is,

It is an act and drama that is being played to earn pity and favors and taking advantage,

It is not, neither need pity nor favors, it is matter of understanding and standing beside during this crisis,

Offering emotional and other essential support, because it is not physically crippling but a mentally crippling stage.

It cannot be seen, it cannot be felt, and it cannot be understood, to the majority it is beyond their imagination,

It was once a brightly shining mind, just as suddenly as diagnosed with incurable cancer, it is an incurable illness, lifelong medication is mandatory,

Nobody in sane mind would want it, it is much more a reality-distorting electrochemical reaction,

Not crept inside due to misuse of drugs or any other vices, but it was printed and mutated inside genes, and it is hereditary.

Bike

When years were a hundred thousand years ago, man was made for woman, and a woman for man,

They were made for each other, what were the designs of God was not known,

Then came the metals, and those were seemingly made for man, exclusive for him, as an exclusive melody from a musician,

Now they became made for each other, but the desire for women did not diminish to possess as his own.

There were too many parameters, factors for man to bond with a woman of his choice,

But metals made it easy when it turned to a machine and engine, near equivalent to a woman, for needs emotional and physical,

Maybe God created man and woman to be with each other, but man alone made a machine for himself, to rejoice,

The machines and engines were only too eager to please man, it was not a woman, but still somewhat whimsical.

When a woman desires a position that pleasures her most, she spreads her legs over man, never termed as improperly,

When a man desires a position that pleasures him most, he spreads his legs over his machine, then goes off like a gunshot,

As a woman possessed over a man, that woman didn't disappoint, so did the machine respond eagerly,

To the stimulation of a man on throttle, as a woman responds to stimulation of clitoris and G-spot.

They had a wild session, the man and the woman, they had a wild session, the machine and man, true motorist,

As the woman entwine a man in peak of physical ecstasy, the machine responded between his crotch, sensation sublime,

What would a man choose? A woman prone to her moods, whereas the machine reacts to even slight response to his wrist?

True liberation it is when the wind blasts on face at 348 kmph, could a woman do that? The point is, with a bike, it is every time.

Verses Without Explanation

Stages. The Amusement and Regret Loop

Actions and aspirations, deeds and desires—if not every one of them—undertaken and held at the age of ten shall be bemusing, redundant, and downright embarrassing at the age of twenty, to the point of regret that something better could or ought to have been done.

Get the drift and keep going in incremental values of ten years.

Actions and aspirations, deeds and desires—if not every one of them—undertaken and held at the age of fifty shall be bemusing, redundant, and downright embarrassing at the age of sixty, to the point of regret that something better could or ought to have been done.

Crystal Ball Gazing

What today the children hear and see, a nation shall tomorrow act and be.

Not Able to Fill the Empty Spaces. A Mind Unfit for Idleness

It is a pathetic state for a person when he is frustrated, genuinely concerned, or puzzled and asks himself: What am I going to do? What should I do? I don't know what to do? —when he has idle or leisure time.

Ideology of Hatred in Democracy. Majority Rule or Majority Rage?

In a country ruled by an iron-fisted dictator, there is no sense in talking about ideology. It is the ideology of a single person or a fringe group forced down the throats of his countrymen.

But in a democracy, it is a matter of principle and just causes that should be maintained.

If a party announces that it has become the majority because the people accept its ideology, it is only a partial truth.

The other part of the ugly truth is that the party has effectively pooled the collective hatred boiling inside the masses. It also awakens the hatred that has been lying dormant on the surface of their consciousness.

They Do See You. Felt Not Said

Mostly, it is the other person's capability to understand your state of mind that is more effective than your attempts to explain or share it.

Omnipresent Caveat. Truths with Asterisks

Everything in life that happens to you comes with a caveat.

Caveat.

There are exceptions. This also proves that a caveat is needed for the above statement. A classic example of an exception is a mother's love for her children.

Stressed Mode and Relaxed Mode

The proper functioning of your brain, especially in work related to earning money, depends on these two modes. A limited amount of stress is necessary to perform efficiently.

But stress cannot be measured. You cannot draw a line and say, this amount of stress is needed for me to function efficiently or this is too much and will lead to burnout. Stress is applied to you; you do not generate it.

On the other hand, when you are in a relaxed state, you can control stress at will. You can dictate the level of stress needed to function efficiently. However, you must be cautious of complacency in this stage.

A Voiceless Self

One self says, Push. Push harder.

Another self says, Quit. Give up.

Between these two selves, there is one self that remains voiceless, thinking: Nobody is asking you to quit. The only thing needed is to slow down.

The self is an individual person as the object of its own reflective consciousness. Since the self is a reference by a subject to itself, this reference is necessarily subjective. This awareness is directed outward from the subject, only to reflect inward—back to its "self."

FAQs

Feverishly or Fervently Asked Questions.

It is strange that there is no limit to the number of nonsenses and truths in this world.

Nonsense being in abundance is somewhat understandable.

But why are there so many versions of truth? Why are so many versions of truth fanatically forced as the truth?

Do You Know What You Want?

The top reasons for fumbling and confusion in decision making is being unsure of what you want.

Yes, It Is Unfortunate

Regretfully, it has to be accepted that grief and sorrow are more powerful emotions than happiness and joy.

More than anything else, they push a man to his most vulnerable state or self.

One of the Many Many Alternatives

When you set your mind, you achieve what you want.

When you are determined you reach the status you aspire.

Then why not aim, set your mind, your determination to earn an epithet,

This guy is fun to be with.

This guy is funny, so I want to be with him.

This will wipe out most of the maladies plaguing the world.

What's Missing? Numbers Don't Wrinkle

You don't age in numbers.

You simply have lost the spirit of youth.

The best part is you can rediscover it.

Importance of Idleness. The Forgotten Virtue of Doing Nothing

Just show the same amount of sincerity when you are searching for the meaning of life to find out the meaning of being idle/idleness.

~ It's a pity that this has to be said.

What You Are When You Have Passed Away. The Vanishing Point

After you have closed your eyes for one final time, we do not know where you are or what you have become, but you have just become an abstract memory within us—and that too, fading fast as time goes by.

That's all you are worth now for us.

Being Idle Above a Certain Age

When was the last time you sat idle, just like when you were a kid—alone, without disturbances, for 30 to 45 minutes in a day?

If You Care for Your Mind and Heart. Checkmate and Tears

Playing chess is good for your mind.

Weeping is good for your heart.

Are you even able to do that anymore?

Mental Illness. The Fractured Deck

When so many things are happening, and with so many thoughts, what makes reality for a normal person is like shuffling a deck of cards. When spread out, it takes a normal pattern that can be understood and is usually sane.

For a mentally ill person, the shuffling of the deck of cards spreads out with a crazy, distorted pattern—and the pattern is different every time and insane.

Just Like That

Quite literally.

If you keep tricking your mind into doing something or not doing something, you are only fooling yourself.

Please Lose Your Cool

It isn't supposed to be that way. It has to come out. Losing your cool is directly linked to the seriousness of an issue or a situation.

Matter of Concern

It is of concern what you have in life and what you don't have in life.

But foremost, if you can't tell for sure within yourself what you want from life, then it is more of a concern than the former two.

Many Those Who Are Better

One of the best ways to avoid making a fool of yourself may not be by becoming more intelligent or smarter, but simply by accepting the fact that there are lots of people who are smarter and more intelligent than you.

Children of Lesser God. Running Without Legs, Seeing Without Eyes

Mental Illness

Asking a mentally ill person to compete and survive in a real-world scenario is like asking a blind man to be a critic of paintings or a movie, or like asking a man affected by polio in his legs to compete in a race to climb the stairs or run a 100-meter dash.

Mental Illness

Inability. Not Won't. Can't.

It's not that he won't, but he just can't.

Useless in every bit of walk of life.

What Is More Important?

Forget about understanding the world in general for a moment. Have you understood your world in the first place?

The One Who Has Lost It All

Hand-me-downs shall be equally humiliating for the one who has more than enough for himself and for the one who once had more than enough but has lost every penny of it.

Color Blind. Nature's Divide, Humanity's Choice

Nature itself has created inequalities by birth in humanity and has also planted a feeling called prejudice. It can also be said that nature is inclined to variety, but did it not create humanity in four broad varieties of color by birth?

Black, White, Brown, and Yellow.

But it has also given humanity compassion, love, and logic. With these, we can surely become color-blind or color-agnostic.

A FOSSianist Way of Life

A FOSSianist doesn't try to find his inner self or something called his soul. Instead, he always strives to be aware of his responsibilities.

Because that is his inner self and soul.

Never Learning from History. An Old Tale or a Stale Tale

There is a huge chunk of humanity, approximately 98%, that wants to go from being happy to becoming happier.

Then there is a tiny chunk of humanity, approximately 2%, that wants to go from being greedy to greedier.

History has evidence that both categories have existed since the beginning of humanity itself.

A Small Nudge

When you are saturated with all good things, you might develop a tendency toward an unknown, unexplainable disinterest.

Getting away from all of it for a short while to a harsher reality can bring back the interest or at least make you appreciate all of your good things.

Ing Dynasty

And in the meanwhile, in the Ing dynasty, a group of intergalactic students met Ms. Makessense. They had chosen the subjects they wanted to pursue and asked her what the cost of education would be.

What is the cost to gain knowledge?

She said, "Here, we don't charge anything to impart knowledge. Knowledge has to be free. You have the option to pay as you please for the time spent by knowledge teachers. Or, if you are well settled in the future, you can pay what you please to pass on this benefit to other students."

"It makes a lot of sense, Ms. Makessense."

"It is," she nodded.

Then she asked two particular students, above eighteen years of age, if they would go out with her. When they consented, she took them to a swanky bar and recreational cannabis smoking club.

Bending the Time

Time has been constant for the past several million years. Sixty seconds is one minute, and 365 days is one year, and so on.

But God has given you the mental ability to bend time. Yes, you have that stupendous ability to bend time. Stretching one minute into an hour, one hour into a day, and so on.

That mental ability is your impatience.

And the side effect of bending time is that you will get irritated and annoyed.

Drying Up of the Well of Tears

As you put more years into your life, it seems like the tears in your eyes are drying up.

Is it because of wisdom and experience or the hardening of your heart?

I think it is the former two.

In Search of Relief

If you are constantly getting irritated, annoyed, or frustrated, it may not always be due to circumstances.

Recalibrate your impatience quotient, and it may offer some relief.

Appear. Breathe Easy. Disappear.

Reality isn't as bad or as worse as you think it is.
It is really the protests of your mind that spoil it.

Bloated Senses

If you feel that you are not appreciated enough for your deeds or work, it may be that for others, it is just routine day's work.

It may also be a by-product of thinking too much of yourself.

Seepage (Irony and Sarcasm)

You need not invade a country or carry a sword to slowly infiltrate an ideology into the masses and ultimately impose fanatical extremism.

The liberal, broad-minded, progressive, tolerant, and humanity-based masses of that country shall make it happen in due course.

FAQs

Can you justify instances of evil by saying, "Oh! There is much good happening elsewhere and everywhere"?

Stress Reliever

When attempting an action, performing a task, or reviewing a decision, there are two ways to approach it:

I hope I am doing everything right.
Is there something that I am doing wrong?
The former shall be less stressful.

The Right Way

There are no persons who can be called good for nothing.
There are always persons who can be called good for something.

Derivative Life

If you really sit down and think, you will realize that, except in your youth, you are doing almost everything for others rather than for yourself.

So He Says and So She Says

Who is better? A son or a daughter?
For a father, a daughter is better. So he says.
For a mother, even though anything is better, a son is better. So she says.

Nine-Pin Bowling

Death plays nine-pin bowling differently.
It knocks down one by one of those who are close to you; father, mother, brother, sister, uncles, aunts . . .
And it always wins. And you always lose.

Mistakes and Corrections

A mistake doesn't appear to be a mistake because you don't realize that it is a mistake.

A mistake doesn't appear to be a mistake because they don't realize that it is a mistake.

So, for #1 - will you yourself realize, accept, correct, and change if you realize that you have made a mistake?

So, for #2 - will you realize, accept, correct, and change even if they don't point out that it is a mistake?

Small Pleasures

After much deliberation, you finally do it.

Then comes the relief and satisfaction, and you say to yourself, I am so glad I did it.

Theirs and Yours

Accepting a person as they are depends on their character and personality and also depends on your character and personality.

Face Value

Increasingly start looking at the mirror, and you shall appear beautiful to your eyes.

Decreasingly start looking at the mirror, and you shall appear beautiful to your mind.

63.84%

I don't feel comfortable; I feel uneasy in the midst of the rich and the super-rich.

I don't feel comfortable; I feel uneasy in the midst of the poor and the very poor.

I don't feel comfortable; I feel uneasy in the midst of the highly intelligent.

I don't feel comfortable; I feel uneasy in the midst of the highly stupid.

For on a 100% scale, I am a 63.84% person.

Soliloquy

It is easier said than done to wish away the guilt and regret after that unpardonable act.

You try to repent, but remorse relentlessly pursues you day after day. You can only steal moments of happiness in between those constant bouts.

Some things are like that, and you will get freedom only when you breathe your last.

Freedom only when you breathe your last? Sadly, it is a yes.

Ing Dynasty

And in the meantime, in the Ing-Dynasty, this was the way of life as often quoted by Ms. Makessense.

Indulgence is a necessary part of life.

Anyway, it shall wane, when you've had too much of it, or as your body and mind age, or when you're just plain weary of it.

Ing Dynasty

So, in the meanwhile in the Ing-Dynasty, Ms. Makessense says thus:

In a Not So Distant Future.

Pop a pill and you shall no longer be hungry for the day.

Pop a pill and you shall taste different food in their best of aroma and taste.

Pop a pill and you shall get all the nutrients for your body and brain.

Pop a pill and you shall attain utmost pleasure for as long you want.

Pop a pill and you shall get a baby of your preferred gender.

Pop a pill and you shall feel all your internal organs repair itself.

Pop a pill and you shall have instant peace and contentment.

Pop a pill and you shall in an instant fall asleep and dream a dream that you have chosen.

Pop a pill and you shall die in a most satisfied and pleasurable manner.

So, for now you know you have appeared. Now breathe easy and disappear.

Appear. Breathe Easy. Disappear.

While you are in pursuit of anything, anything at all, a good house, a top position in a corporation, or climbing the highest mountains, you will experience many emotions: thrill, anticipation, happiness. But not these two:

Peace and contentment.

Corollary:

The day you stop pursuing anything and simply exist; you shall have peace and contentment.

Note:

You should have these basics secured: food, clothing, shelter, financial stability, and, most importantly, health.

In the Ing-Dynasty, these are all taken care of from cradle to coffin, without pursuit.

Ing-Dynasty

First of Fundamentals.

And in the meanwhile, in the Ing-Dynasty, Ms. Makessense theorizes thus:

Theorem: There can never be equality in humanity.

A smaller group always sows the seeds of inequality, time and time again, across countless cycles, driven by an inbuilt nature of greed and self-serving needs. A slightly larger group fights back in a futile attempt to restore even a semblance of equality for the much, much larger group, the entirety of humanity.

The small group always succeeds.

The comparatively larger group always tries.

The much, much larger group, the entirety of humanity, always wallows in misery.

Ms. Makessense's theorem in the Ing-Dynasty suggests that this cycle is fundamental, as if an immutable law of existence. The irony lies in the predictability of the pattern: despite constant struggle, inequality is never eradicated, only rearranged.

Mental Illness

Mental illness is the constant shifting between blocks of time, ranging from a day to a week, to a month, to a year, wondering: Who am I? What is my reality? Or, for that matter, what is reality itself inside my head? Yet, despite this relentless uncertainty, I wear a smile and a mask of normalcy on my face.

A Gentle Man

A man is, by nature, an animal.

A gentleman is one who never allows his animal instincts to surface; whether by nature or through sheer will and strength of character.

Verses With Explanation

Stages. The Amusement and Regret Loop.

Actions and aspirations, deeds and desires, if not every one of them, undertaken and held at the age of ten shall be bemusing, redundant, and downright embarrassing at the age of twenty, to the point of regret that something better could or ought to have been done.

Get the drift and keep going in incremental values of ten years.

Actions and aspirations, deeds and desires, if not every one of them, undertaken and held at the age of fifty shall be bemusing, redundant, and downright embarrassing at the age of sixty, to the point of regret that something better could or ought to have been done.

Explanation:

This passage illustrates how each stage of life renders the previous one outdated or even regrettable. What once seemed reasonable or meaningful at ten becomes a source of amusement or embarrassment at twenty. The pattern continues with every decade, reinforcing the idea that each stage judges the last with the thought that something better could or ought to have been done.

Crystal Ball Gazing

What today the children hear and see, a nation shall tomorrow act and be.

Explanation:

This passage encapsulates the profound influence of childhood experiences on the future of a nation. The beliefs, values, and ideas instilled in children today shape the decisions and actions of society tomorrow. It suggests that a nation's destiny is not written in policies alone but in the collective consciousness formed during youth.

By emphasizing "hear and see," the passage underscores how exposure to information, culture, and societal norms molds future generations. It serves as both a reflection and a caution, highlighting the responsibility of shaping young minds wisely, as they will inevitably shape the world in return.

Not Able to Fill the Empty Spaces. A Mind Unfit for Idleness.

It is a pathetic state for a person when he is frustrated, genuinely concerned, or puzzled and asks himself: What am I going to do? What should I do? I don't know what to do, when he has idle or leisure time.

Explanation:

This passage highlights the irony of leisure becoming a source of distress rather than enjoyment. Free time should be a period of relaxation and fulfillment, yet some find themselves lost, unable to embrace it. Instead of appreciating leisure, they are consumed by uncertainty, as if time itself demands an immediate purpose.

The passage suggests that such a state is not just unfortunate but pitiable, exposing an inability to simply be at ease. It serves as a reflection on modern life, where constant activity is expected, and stillness feels unnatural rather than something to be savored.

Ideology of Hatred in Democracy. Majority Rule or Majority Rage?

In a country ruled by an iron-fisted dictator, there is no sense in talking about ideology. It is the ideology of a single person or a fringe group forced down the throats of his countrymen.

But in a democracy, it is a matter of principle and just causes that should be maintained.

If a party announces that it has become the majority because the people accept its ideology, it is only a partial truth.

The other part of the ugly truth is that the party has effectively pooled the collective hatred boiling inside the masses. It also awakens the hatred that has been lying dormant on the surface of their consciousness.

Explanation:

In a dictatorship, ideology is imposed without discussion. In a democracy, ideology is meant to be rooted in principles and just causes. However, the passage exposes a darker reality; political success is often not just about public support but also about mobilizing existing resentments. A ruling party may claim legitimacy based on ideological acceptance, but it also capitalizes on deep-seated animosities, bringing dormant hatreds to the surface. The passage critiques how democracy, while appearing free and fair, can be manipulated through fear and division, making hatred a powerful political tool rather than an unintended consequence.

They Do See You. Felt Not Said.

Mostly, it is the other person's capability to understand your state of mind that is more effective than your attempts to explain or share it.

Explanation:

This passage reflects on the power of perception over verbal expression. It suggests that true understanding does not always come from explaining oneself but from the listener's ability to grasp another's mental state. Some emotions, struggles, or inner conflicts are beyond words, and a perceptive person can recognize them without needing an explanation. This highlights the importance of empathy and emotional intelligence—understanding is not just about what is said but about what is felt and observed.

Omnipresent Caveat. Truths with Asterisks.

Everything in life that happens to you comes with a caveat.

Caveat.

There are exceptions. This also proves that a caveat is needed for the above statement. A classic example of an exception is a mother's love for her children.

Explanation:

This passage plays with the concept of self-referential logic—if everything in life comes with a caveat, then even this statement requires one. It highlights the complexity of absolute truths, showing that exceptions are an inherent part of any rule. The mention of a mother's love serves as a counterpoint, suggesting that some aspects of human experience transcend conditions and limitations. The passage cleverly critiques the tendency to generalize, reminding us that even the most seemingly universal truths are not without exceptions.

Stressed Mode and Relaxed Mode

The proper functioning of your brain, especially in work related to earning money, depends on these two modes. A limited amount of stress is necessary to perform efficiently.

But stress cannot be measured. You cannot draw a line and say, this amount of stress is needed for me to function efficiently or this is too much and will lead to burnout. Stress is applied to you; you do not generate it.

On the other hand, when you are in a relaxed state, you can control stress at will. You can dictate the level of stress needed to function efficiently. However, you must be cautious of complacency in this stage.

Explanation:

This passage explores the delicate balance between stress and relaxation in maintaining productivity. Stress, when externally imposed, is unpredictable and can either enhance efficiency or lead to burnout. Since it cannot be precisely measured, individuals often struggle to find the right balance. Conversely, in a relaxed state, one has the ability to regulate stress, making it a tool rather than a burden. However, the danger of relaxation lies in complacency—if one becomes too comfortable, the drive to perform may diminish. The passage ultimately suggests that neither extreme is ideal; rather, awareness and control over these states are key to sustained productivity.

A Voiceless Self

One self says, Push. Push harder.

Another self says, Quit. Give up.

Between these two selves, there is one self that remains voiceless, thinking: Nobody is asking you to quit. The only thing needed is to slow down.

The self is an individual person as the object of its own reflective consciousness. Since the self is a reference by a subject to itself, this reference is necessarily subjective. This awareness is directed outward from the subject, only to reflect inward—back to its "self."

Explanation:

This passage explores the internal conflict between ambition and surrender, highlighting a third, often-overlooked state: the voiceless self. While one part of us pushes for relentless effort and another urges retreat, the silent self merely seeks balance—it does not wish to quit but only to slow down. The passage then delves into the philosophical nature of the self, emphasizing its inherently subjective and recursive nature. The self is both observer and observed, constantly oscillating between external pressures and internal reflection.

FAQs.

Feverishly or Fervently Asked Questions.

It is strange that there is no limit to the number of nonsenses and truths in this world.

Nonsense being in abundance is somewhat understandable.

But why are there so many versions of truth? Why are so many versions of truth fanatically forced as the truth?

Explanation:

This passage questions the nature of truth and its multiplicity. While the abundance of nonsense is expected, the perplexing aspect is the existence of countless versions of "truth"—each often presented with unwavering conviction. The passage subtly critiques dogmatism, pointing out that many people impose their interpretation of truth as the absolute one. This raises deeper philosophical inquiries: Is truth subjective? Or is it simply fragmented by individual perception, bias, and belief systems?

Do You Know What You Want?

The top reasons for fumbling and confusion in decision making is being unsure of what you want.

Explanation:

This passage highlights the fundamental cause of indecision—uncertainty about one's own desires. When a person lacks clarity about what they truly want, choices become overwhelming, and hesitation follows. The passage implies that decision-making is not just about weighing options but about first understanding one's own goals and priorities. Without this self-awareness, every choice feels like a gamble rather than a step forward.

Yes, It Is Unfortunate.

Regretfully, it has to be accepted that grief and sorrow are more powerful emotions than happiness and joy.

More than anything else, they push a man to his most vulnerable state or self.

Explanation:

This passage reflects on the overwhelming power of negative emotions compared to positive ones. Grief and sorrow have a depth and intensity that often surpass the fleeting nature of happiness. While joy uplifts, sorrow has the ability to break, reshape, and redefine a person, exposing their most vulnerable self. The passage does not merely acknowledge this truth but also conveys a quiet resignation—an acceptance that, despite our desires, suffering holds greater influence over the human experience.

One of the Many, Many Alternatives

When you set your mind, you achieve what you want.

When you are determined, you reach the status you aspire.

Then why not aim, set your mind, your determination to earn an epithet:

This guy is fun to be with.

This guy is funny, so I want to be with him.

This will wipe out most of the maladies plaguing the world.

Explanation:

This musing proposes a subtle but profound alternative to conventional life goals. Rather than aspiring to power, wealth, or fame, it suggests striving to be someone others genuinely enjoy being around—light-hearted, humorous, and pleasant. The idea is that if more people made being enjoyable company their goal, it would dissolve much of the aggression, loneliness, and conflict that afflict society. Laughter and warmth, often undervalued, are offered here as potent tools for social healing. A redefinition of success not in material terms, but in emotional resonance.

What's Missing? Numbers Don't Wrinkle.

You don't age in numbers.

You simply have lost the spirit of youth.

The best part is you can rediscover it.

Explanation:

This thought challenges the conventional view of aging as a mere accumulation of years. Instead, it suggests that aging is the result of losing the vitality, curiosity, and enthusiasm associated with youth. The good news is that this youthful spirit is not permanently lost—it can be rekindled through perspective, action, and mindset. It invites the reader to consider how their perception of aging might be self-imposed rather than inevitable, urging them to reclaim a sense of wonder and engagement with life.

Importance of Idleness. The Forgotten Virtue of Doing Nothing.

Just show the same amount of sincerity when you are searching for the meaning of life to find out the meaning of being idle/idleness.

~ It's a pity that this has to be said.

Explanation:

This thought highlights the paradox in how people pursue meaning. Many tirelessly search for a grand purpose but fail to recognize the value of stillness, rest, and idleness. The phrase "it's a pity that this has to be said" suggests a cultural bias against idleness, as if its worth should be self-evident. The passage challenges the reader to reconsider their assumptions: Could idleness itself be meaningful? Does our obsession with productivity blind us to the wisdom found in quiet, unstructured moments?

What You Are When You Have Passed Away. The Vanishing Point.

After you have closed your eyes for one final time, we do not know where you are or what you have become, but you have just become an abstract memory within us—and that too, fading fast as time goes by.

That's all you are worth now for us.

Explanation:

This passage presents a stark, unsentimental view of death. It acknowledges the great unknown—what happens after death—while focusing on the undeniable reality: once gone, a person exists only in the memories of others, which inevitably fade with time. The final sentence delivers a blunt truth: no matter how significant one's life may have seemed, in the eyes of the living, they become nothing more than a transient recollection. It forces the reader to confront their own mortality and the fleeting nature of human legacy.

Being Idle Above a Certain Age

When was the last time you sat idle, just like when you were a kid—alone, without disturbances, for 30 to 45 minutes in a day?

Explanation:

This thought provokes reflection on how modern adulthood often eliminates true idleness. As children, we could sit in silence, daydream, or simply exist without an agenda. But as we grow older, responsibilities, distractions, and the pressure to be "productive" erode this simple practice. The question challenges the reader to recognize how rare and possibly valuable such moments have become. It implies that reclaiming idleness might restore something essential—perhaps clarity, creativity, or inner peace.

If You Care for Your Mind and Heart. Checkmate and Tears.

Playing chess is good for your mind.

Weeping is good for your heart.

Are you even able to do that anymore?

Explanation:

This passage juxtaposes two contrasting yet essential human experiences: intellectual stimulation and emotional release. Chess symbolizes mental exercise—strategy, patience, and problem-solving—while weeping represents emotional depth and vulnerability. The final question challenges the reader: Have they lost touch with these fundamental aspects of their being? In a world that often prioritizes efficiency over introspection, many may find themselves incapable of deep thought or genuine emotional expression. This thought serves as both an observation and a quiet provocation.

Mental Illness. The Fractured Deck.

When so many things are happening, and with so many thoughts, what makes reality for a normal person is like shuffling a deck of cards. When spread out, it takes a normal pattern that can be understood and is usually sane.

For a mentally ill person, the shuffling of the deck of cards spreads out with a crazy, distorted pattern—and the pattern is different every time and insane.

Explanation:

This thought presents mental illness as a chaotic distortion of perception and cognition. A healthy mind, like a shuffled deck of cards, still follows an order that can be reconstructed and understood. In contrast, a mentally ill mind experiences a reality that is unpredictable, fragmented, and ever-changing, making coherence elusive. The metaphor of shuffling highlights how randomness and instability replace the expected structure, conveying the disorienting nature of mental illness to those who may not have experienced it firsthand.

Just Like That

Quite literally

If you keep tricking your mind into doing something or not doing something, you are only fooling yourself.

Explanation:

This thought exposes the illusion of self-deception. Many people convince themselves they can override desires, fears, or habits through mental tricks. Whether it's suppressing emotions, forcing motivation, or avoiding reality, the act of tricking oneself doesn't work that well. The phrase "quite literally" reinforces the blunt truth: you can play mental games, but you are always the player and the played.

Please Lose Your Cool

It isn't supposed to be that way. It has to come out. Losing your cool is directly linked to the seriousness of an issue or a situation.

Explanation:

This thought challenges the conventional wisdom that staying calm is always ideal. It argues that anger, frustration, or an emotional outburst is sometimes necessary—an honest reaction to something deeply significant. Suppressing emotions can create an illusion of control, but in reality, some things demand a visceral response. The phrase "it has to come out" suggests that emotions, when repressed, don't disappear; they accumulate. This idea reframes losing one's cool not as weakness but as a natural and sometimes necessary reaction to life's gravity.

Matter of Concern

It is of concern what you have in life and what you don't have in life.

But foremost, if you can't tell for sure within yourself what you want from life, then it is more of a concern than the former two.

Explanation:

This thought highlights a hierarchy of concerns. People often worry about their possessions and what they lack, but the greater issue is not knowing what they truly desire. Without clarity about one's purpose or direction, even abundance or deprivation becomes secondary. It urges the reader to turn their concern inward, questioning whether they have ever truly understood what they seek.

Many Those Who Are Better

One of the best ways to avoid making a fool of yourself may not be by becoming more intelligent or smarter, but simply by accepting the fact that there are lots of people who are smarter and more intelligent than you.

Explanation:

This thought suggests that wisdom doesn't always come from increasing one's intelligence but from recognizing one's limitations. The ego often resists acknowledging the superiority of others, leading to overconfidence and, ultimately, foolishness. The passage reframes intelligence—not as something to prove, but as something to respect in others.

Mental Illness

Children of Lesser God. Running Without Legs, Seeing Without Eyes

Asking a mentally ill person to compete and survive in a real-world scenario is like asking a blind man to be a critic of paintings or a movie, or like asking a man affected by polio in his legs to compete in a race to climb the stairs or run a 100-meter dash.

Explanation:

This thought starkly illustrates the unfair expectations placed on those with mental illness. Society often demands that they function within systems designed for the neurotypical, disregarding the unique challenges they face. The comparisons emphasize the absurdity of such demands—just as physical impairments limit certain abilities, mental struggles create invisible barriers that cannot be willed away. The phrase "Children of Lesser God" evokes a sense of injustice, hinting at the way the mentally ill are often overlooked, misunderstood, or expected to perform on an unequal playing field.

Mental Illness

Inability. Not Won't—Can't.

It's not that he won't, but he just can't.
Useless in every bit of walk of life.

Explanation:

This thought confronts the brutal reality of how mental illness can render a person functionally incapacitated—not from a lack of will, but from a lack of ability. The key distinction lies in the line "he just can't," which dispels the common misconception that mentally ill individuals are lazy or unwilling. The final line is raw, even harsh, reflecting how society—or the person themselves—might perceive their condition. It exposes the deep alienation and helplessness often experienced in mental illness, without softening the truth.

What Is More Important?

Forget about understanding the world in general for a moment.
Have you understood your world in the first place?

Explanation:

This thought redirects the reader's focus inward. Many people strive to grasp the complexities of the world—philosophy, politics, society—without first understanding their own inner workings. It challenges the reader to question whether they have ever truly examined their own thoughts, emotions, and personal reality before attempting to make sense of the larger world.

The One Who Has Lost It All

Hand-me-downs shall be equally humiliating for the one who has more than enough for himself and for the one who once had more than enough but has lost every penny of it.

Explanation:

This thought explores the complex relationship between pride, loss, and perceived dignity. A person who has never struggled financially may find hand-me-downs humiliating due to their accustomed privilege. Likewise, someone who once had wealth but lost everything may feel the sting of being reduced to dependence. The shared humiliation suggests that losing status can be just as painful as never having it in the first place.

Color Blind. Nature's Divide, Humanity's Choice.

Nature itself has created inequalities by birth in humanity and has also planted a feeling called prejudice. It can also be said that nature is inclined to variety, but did it not create humanity in four broad varieties of color by birth?

Black, White, Brown, and Yellow.

But it has also given humanity compassion, love, and logic. With these, we can surely become color-blind or color-agnostic.

Explanation:

This thought presents a paradox: nature itself created differences, yet it also endowed humans with the ability to transcend them. While physical distinctions exist from birth, prejudice is a human construct. The passage suggests that, although nature may categorize, the higher faculties of compassion, love, and logic allow humanity to rise above these divisions. The phrase "color-blind or color-agnostic" proposes two perspectives—one where differences are ignored, and another where they are acknowledged but do not determine worth.

A FOSSianist Way of Life

A FOSSianist doesn't try to find his inner self or something called his soul. Instead, he always strives to be aware of his responsibilities.

Because that is his inner self and soul.

Explanation:

This thought redefines the search for meaning. Unlike traditional introspection, where one seeks an abstract "inner self" or "soul," the FOSSianist sees duty and responsibility as the essence of identity. The passage suggests that who we are is not found through contemplation but through action. Awareness of one's role in life—whether toward others, society, or a cause—becomes the ultimate form of self-realization. This philosophy rejects passive self-discovery in favor of active engagement with the world.

Never Learning from History. An Old Tale or a Stale Tale.

There is a huge chunk of humanity, approximately 98%, that wants to go from being happy to becoming happier.

Then there is a tiny chunk of humanity, approximately 2%, that wants to go from being greedy to greedier.

History has evidence that both categories have existed since the beginning of humanity itself.

Explanation:

This thought highlights the persistence of human nature throughout history. The majority of people seek fulfillment in happiness, always wanting more but within the realm of contentment. A smaller, yet powerful minority, seeks fulfillment in greed—accumulating wealth, power, or influence with no limit. The passage subtly suggests that despite centuries of civilization; these fundamental divisions remain unchanged. The title, "Never Learning from History," implies that society continually repeats the same cycles, unable or unwilling to alter its course.

A Small Nudge

When you are saturated with all good things, you might develop a tendency toward an unknown, unexplainable disinterest.

Getting away from all of it for a short while to a harsher reality can bring back the interest—or at least make you appreciate all of your good things.

Explanation:

This thought speaks to the phenomenon of desensitization—when abundance dulls appreciation. Too much comfort, success, or pleasure can paradoxically lead to boredom or apathy. The suggested solution is contrast: stepping into a harsher reality, even briefly, can rekindle gratitude and restore lost enthusiasm. The phrase "a small nudge" suggests that only a slight shift is needed to reset one's perspective, emphasizing that the remedy isn't deprivation but exposure to life's rawer aspects.

Ing Dynasty

And in the meanwhile, in the Ing dynasty, a group of intergalactic students met Ms. Makessense. They had chosen the subjects they wanted to pursue and asked her what the cost of education would be.

What is the cost to gain knowledge?

She said, "Here, we don't charge anything to impart knowledge. Knowledge has to be free. You have the option to pay as you please for the time spent by knowledge teachers. Or, if you are well settled in the future, you can pay what you please to pass on this benefit to other students."

"It makes a lot of sense, Ms. Makessense."

"It is," she nodded.

Then she asked two particular students, above eighteen years of age, if they would go out with her. When they consented, she took them to a swanky bar and recreational cannabis smoking club.

Explanation:

This surreal, futuristic musing presents an alternate perspective on education—one where knowledge is free, and teachers are compensated based on gratitude rather than fixed fees. The name "Ms. Makessense" plays on the idea of reason and fairness in the way education is structured. The unexpected shift to a bar and cannabis club adds a satirical or ironic twist, questioning the true nature of wisdom and leisure. Does knowledge always lead to seriousness, or can it coexist with indulgence? The passage blends utopian ideals with a touch of irreverence.

Bending the Time

Time has been constant for the past several million years. Sixty seconds is one minute, and 365 days is one year, and so on.

But God has given you the mental ability to bend time. Yes, you have that stupendous ability to bend time—stretching one minute into an hour, one hour into a day, and so on.

That mental ability is your impatience.

And the side effect of bending time is that you will get irritated and annoyed.

Explanation:

This thought explores the subjective nature of time perception. While time itself remains constant, our experience of it is malleable, shaped by our emotions. Impatience warps time, making short waits feel unbearably long, stretching moments of anticipation into eternity. This passage suggests that we are all, in a sense, time manipulators—though at a cost. The consequence of this mental "bending" is frustration, revealing how much of our suffering comes not from external reality but from our perception of it.

Drying Up of the Well of Tears

As you put more years into your life, it seems like the tears in your eyes are drying up.

Is it because of wisdom and experience or the hardening of your heart?

I think it is the former two.

Explanation:

This thought reflects on the diminishing expression of sorrow with age. In youth, emotions often flow freely, but as time passes, tears become rare. The question posed suggests two possibilities: either wisdom and experience have helped one process pain differently, or the heart has grown calloused. The closing line leans toward the gentler explanation, implying that maturity replaces emotional outbursts with quiet understanding. Yet, it leaves room for doubt—does wisdom truly make one stronger, or does it merely make suffering less visible?

In Search of Relief

If you are constantly getting irritated, annoyed, or frustrated, it may not always be due to circumstances.

Recalibrate your impatience quotient, and it may offer some relief.

Explanation:

This thought suggests that frustration isn't always caused by external events but can stem from within. While people often blame their surroundings for irritation, impatience plays a significant role in how they perceive and react to situations. The phrase "recalibrate your impatience quotient" implies that adjusting one's mindset—learning to tolerate delays, uncertainties, and imperfections—can lead to relief. The passage invites introspection, urging the reader to consider whether their distress is truly justified or simply a habit of mind.

Appear. Breathe Easy. Disappear.

Reality isn't as bad or as worse as you think it is.

It is really the protests of your mind that spoil it.

Explanation:

The title suggests a fleeting, effortless way of existing—appearing, breathing easily, and then disappearing. It implies a state of detachment, where one moves through life without unnecessary resistance. Instead of getting entangled in mental protests, frustrations, or over-analysis, one simply "breathes easy" and lets it go. The passage reinforces this idea by suggesting that reality is not inherently harsh; it is the mind's resistance that makes it seem so. The title can be interpreted as an approach to life: embrace the moment, exist without excess struggle, and move on when the time comes.

Bloated Senses

If you feel that you are not appreciated enough for your deeds or work, it may be that for others, it is just routine day's work.

It may also be a by-product of thinking too much of yourself.

Explanation:

This thought challenges the expectation of recognition. What one sees as extraordinary effort might be viewed by others as ordinary, simply because perspectives differ. The phrase "bloated senses" suggests an inflated self-perception—perhaps a tendency to overestimate one's own importance. This isn't necessarily a critique but rather an invitation to reconsider whether the lack of appreciation is due to external indifference or internal exaggeration. A recalibration of expectations might lead to less disappointment and a more balanced sense of self-worth.

Seepage

You need not invade a country or carry a sword to slowly infiltrate an ideology into the masses and ultimately impose fanatical extremism.

The liberal, broad-minded, progressive, tolerant, and humanity-based masses of that country shall make it happen in due course.

Explanation (With Emphasis on Irony & Sarcasm):

This passage delivers a scathing irony: the downfall of a society doesn't always come from external attacks but from within, enabled by those who believe they are protecting it. The people who pride themselves on being tolerant and progressive—who would never dream of imposing anything on anyone—ironically create the perfect conditions for the very extremism they stand against. The sarcasm is in the inevitability implied: why bother with conquest when the door is left wide open? The so-called guardians of broad-mindedness become unwitting facilitators of what they fear most.

FAQs

Can you justify instances of evil by saying, "Oh! There is much good happening elsewhere and everywhere"?

Explanation:

This passage questions a common yet flawed way of thinking—using the presence of good to downplay or excuse evil. While good and evil coexist, acknowledging good does not erase wrongdoing. The phrasing of the question highlights how people sometimes dismiss or ignore suffering by shifting focus to positivity elsewhere, as if that somehow balances the scales. The passage challenges the reader to reflect on whether recognizing goodness should ever serve as a justification for ignoring or excusing evil.

Stress Reliever

When attempting an action, performing a task, or reviewing a decision, there are two ways to approach it:

I hope I am doing everything right.

Is there something that I am doing wrong?

The former shall be less stressful.

Explanation:

This passage highlights the psychological impact of mindset when engaging with tasks or decisions. The first approach (I hope I am doing everything right) carries an implicit trust in one's actions and allows for a smoother, less anxious process. The second approach (Is there something that I am doing wrong?), while useful for self-improvement, invites doubt and self-criticism, potentially leading to unnecessary stress. The thought suggests that focusing on confidence rather than fear of error can serve as a natural stress reliever, making tasks feel less burdensome.

The Right Way

There are no persons who can be called good for nothing.

There are always persons who can be called good for something.

Explanation:

This passage flips a common dismissive phrase on its head, emphasizing that every individual holds some form of value. The first line challenges the idea that anyone is entirely useless, while the second line reframes the perspective—everyone has a purpose, skill, or contribution, even if it isn't immediately recognized. The phrasing offers a subtle yet powerful shift in mindset: instead of labeling people based on their perceived shortcomings, one can choose to see what they bring to the table. It's an invitation to reconsider judgments and appreciate the hidden worth in others.

Derivative Life

If you really sit down and think, you will realize that—except in your youth—you are doing almost everything for others rather than for yourself.

Explanation:

This passage presents a stark reflection on how life's priorities shift over time. In youth, actions are often self-driven—centered around personal dreams, desires, and ambitions. However, as one grows older, responsibilities take over, and much of life becomes about fulfilling obligations to family, society, or work. The phrase "derivative life" suggests that one's actions become less about personal fulfillment and more about serving as a function of others' needs. It's a quiet nudge to reflect on whether this shift is natural, necessary, or something to be questioned.

So He Says and So She Says

Who is better? A son or a daughter?
For a father, a daughter is better. So he says.

For a mother, even though anything is better, a son is better. So she says.

Explanation:

This passage subtly highlights the deep-seated emotional bonds parents have with their children, often shaped by traditional perspectives. The father's preference for a daughter and the mother's preference for a son reflect a pattern seen in many cultures, where daughters are often viewed as closer to their fathers and sons to their mothers. The phrase so he says and so she says adds an element of subjectivity, suggesting that these preferences are not absolute truths but rather shaped by individual experiences, biases, or societal conditioning.

Nine-Pin Bowling

Death plays nine-pin bowling differently.

It knocks down one by one of those who are close to you—father, mother, brother, sister, uncles, aunts . . .

And it always wins. And you always lose.

Explanation:

This passage paints a stark, inevitable reality through the metaphor of a nine-pin bowling game. Unlike regular bowling, where the goal is to knock down all pins at once, death operates slowly and methodically, taking loved ones one by one. The phrase and it always wins. And you always lose. drives home the inescapability of mortality—no matter how much we cherish those around us, loss is certain. The simplicity of the imagery makes the reflection all the more haunting, emphasizing the quiet cruelty of time.

Mistakes and Corrections

A mistake doesn't appear to be a mistake because you don't realize that it is a mistake.

A mistake doesn't appear to be a mistake because they don't realize that it is a mistake.

So, for #1—will you yourself realize, accept, correct, and change if you realize that you have made a mistake?

So, for #2—will you realize, accept, correct, and change even if they don't point out that it is a mistake?

Explanation:

This passage plays with two perspectives on mistakes—self-awareness and external validation. The first statement suggests that one's own ignorance of an error prevents correction. The second suggests that a mistake might persist simply because others fail to recognize it. The challenge posed by the questions highlights personal responsibility: Are you capable of change without being told? And more importantly, are you willing to correct yourself even when no one is watching?

Small Pleasures

After much deliberation, you finally do it.

Then comes the relief and satisfaction, and you say to yourself—I am so glad I did it.

Explanation:

This passage captures the quiet yet profound joy that comes from overcoming hesitation. The "it" remains deliberately vague, allowing the reader to project their own experiences onto the statement—whether it's making a difficult decision, completing a task, or taking a long-overdue action. The delayed gratification of finally acting after internal debate makes the relief sweeter. It emphasizes how even small victories can bring immense satisfaction, reinforcing the idea that action, no matter how minor, often brings more peace than prolonged hesitation.

Theirs and Yours

Accepting a person as they are depends on their character and personality and also depends on your character and personality.

Explanation:

This passage highlights the dual nature of acceptance. People often think that whether they accept someone is based solely on the other person's qualities—whether they are likable, kind, or trustworthy. However, the statement points out that acceptance is also a reflection of the one doing the accepting. Your own biases, experiences, and temperament shape how you perceive others. It subtly suggests that true acceptance is as much about yourself as it is about the other person's traits.

Face Value

Increasingly start looking at the mirror, and you shall appear beautiful to your eyes.

Decreasingly start looking at the mirror, and you shall appear beautiful to your mind.

Explanation:

This passage plays on the duality of external and internal beauty. The first statement suggests that frequent exposure to one's own reflection breeds familiarity, making one more accepting (or even admiring) of their physical appearance. The second statement flips the idea—stepping away from the mirror shifts focus inward, allowing the mind to redefine beauty beyond mere looks.

63.84%

I don't feel comfortable; I feel uneasy in the midst of the rich and the super-rich.

I don't feel comfortable; I feel uneasy in the midst of the poor and the very poor.

I don't feel comfortable; I feel uneasy in the midst of the highly intelligent.

I don't feel comfortable; I feel uneasy in the midst of the highly stupid.

For on a 100% scale, I am a 63.84% person.

Explanation:

This passage reflects the discomfort of feeling out of place among extremes—whether of wealth or intelligence. The narrator experiences unease both among the affluent and the impoverished, as well as among the highly intelligent and the less so. The specific figure, 63.84%, humorously suggests a self-assessment of being moderately above average, yet not aligning with any extreme group. This sentiment underscores the challenge of finding a sense of belonging when one perceives themselves as residing in the middle ground, neither identifying with the peaks nor the valleys of societal measures.

Soliloquy

It is easier said than done to wish away the guilt and regret after that unpardonable act.

You try to repent, but remorse relentlessly pursues you day after day. You can only steal moments of happiness in between those constant bouts.

Some things are like that, and you will get freedom only when you breathe your last.

Freedom only when you breathe your last? Sadly, it is a yes.

Explanation:

This passage delves into the inescapable nature of profound guilt and remorse. The narrator acknowledges the challenge of dismissing these emotions following an unforgivable act. Despite attempts at repentance, remorse becomes a persistent shadow, allowing only fleeting moments of happiness. The contemplation that true liberation from such torment comes only with death underscores the depth of their anguish. This introspective soliloquy highlights the human struggle with self-forgiveness and the heavy burden of carrying unresolved guilt throughout one's life.

Ing Dynasty

And in the meantime, in the Ing-Dynasty, this was the way of life as often quoted by Ms. Makessense.

Indulgence is a necessary part of life.

Anyway, it shall wane—when you've had too much of it, or as your body and mind age, or when you're just plain weary of it.

Explanation:

Set in a fictional or symbolic place—the "Ing-Dynasty"—this musing conveys a dry, reflective truth about indulgence. Through Ms. Makessense, a fittingly named voice of reason, the piece suggests that indulgence is not something to be vilified. In fact, it is essential, even inevitable, in human life. The irony lies in its self-regulating nature: indulgence fades not because of moral superiority or discipline, but through fatigue, saturation, or the biological decline of interest. The message subtly pokes fun at asceticism while asserting a grounded acceptance of human tendencies.

Ing Dynasty

So, in the meanwhile in the Ing-Dynasty, Ms. Makessense says thus:

In a Not So Distant Future.

Pop a pill and you shall no longer be hungry for the day.

Pop a pill and you shall taste different food in their best of aroma and taste.

Pop a pill and you shall get all the nutrients for your body and brain.

Pop a pill and you shall attain utmost pleasure for as long you want.

Pop a pill and you shall get a baby of your preferred gender.

Pop a pill and you shall feel all your internal organs repair itself.

Pop a pill and you shall have instant peace and contentment.

Pop a pill and you shall in an instant fall asleep and dream a dream that you have chosen.

Pop a pill and you shall die in a most satisfied and pleasurable manner.

So, for now you have appeared. Now breathe easy and disappear.

Explanation:

This verse envisions a jaw-dropping future made possible by staggering scientific and technological advancements. Each "pop a pill" line showcases how effortlessly humanity might someday achieve what once took effort, time, and emotional cost—eating, healing, feeling pleasure, procreation, peace, and even death. It is a compact yet powerful statement about humanity's march toward convenience through innovation. Rather than mock it, the tone marvels at its possibility. The phrase "breathe easy and disappear" elegantly echoes the entire idea: you arrive, experience existence with the help of technology, and vanish—quietly, smoothly, with nothing left unresolved.

Appear. Breathe Easy. Disappear.

While you are in pursuit of anything—anything at all—a good house, a top position in a corporation, or climbing the highest mountains, you will experience many emotions: thrill, anticipation, happiness. But not these two:

Peace and contentment.

Corollary:

The day you stop pursuing anything and simply exist; you shall have peace and contentment.

Note:

You should have these basics secured: food, clothing, shelter, financial stability, and, most importantly, health.

In the Ing-Dynasty, these are all taken care of from cradle to coffin—without pursuit.

Explanation:

This piece examines the relationship between ambition and inner peace. It suggests that as long as one is striving for something—whether material success, status, or adventure—certain emotions will arise, but peace and contentment will remain elusive. True tranquility, it argues, comes only when one ceases to chase after things and simply exist. The footnotes reinforce that basic survival needs must be met for this state to be possible. The Ing-Dynasty reference introduces a futuristic utopia where everything is effortlessly provided, hinting at a world where struggle is obsolete.

Ing-Dynasty

First of Fundamentals.

And in the meanwhile, in the Ing-Dynasty, Ms. Makessense theorizes thus:

Theorem: There can never be equality in humanity.

A smaller group always sows the seeds of inequality—time and time again, across countless cycles—driven by an inbuilt nature of greed and self-serving needs. A slightly larger group fights back in a futile attempt to restore even a semblance of equality for the much, much larger group—the entirety of humanity.

The small group always succeeds.
The comparatively larger group always tries.
The much, much larger group—the entirety of humanity—always wallows in misery.

Explanation:

This passage presents a stark and deterministic view of human society, where true equality is deemed impossible. The argument rests on the premise that greed is an intrinsic trait of a select few, who continuously manipulate power structures to maintain their dominance. Meanwhile, a slightly larger opposition group struggles—futilely—to resist this imbalance, never truly overturning it. The majority, the common people, remain trapped in an endless cycle of exploitation and suffering.

Ms. Makessense's theorem in the Ing-Dynasty suggests that this cycle is fundamental, as if an immutable law of existence. The irony lies in the predictability of the pattern: despite constant struggle, inequality is never eradicated, only rearranged.

Mental Illness

Mental illness is the constant shifting between blocks of time—ranging from a day to a week, to a month, to a year—wondering: Who am I? What is my reality? Or, for that matter, what is reality itself inside my head? Yet, despite this relentless uncertainty, I wear a smile and a mask of normalcy on my face.

Explanation:

This passage captures the isolating and disorienting experience of mental illness. The shifting timeframes emphasize the unpredictable nature of the condition—some days may feel lucid, while others dissolve into confusion. The central struggle is not just an external one but an internal battle against a fractured sense of self and reality.

The irony is in the contrast: while the mind is in turmoil, the external world sees only a composed, smiling face. This duality speaks to the silent suffering of many who live with mental illness, maintaining an illusion of normalcy while grappling with existential uncertainty. It also raises a profound question—if reality itself feels unstable, can one ever truly define their own existence?

A Gentle Man

A man is, by nature, an animal.

A gentleman is one who never allows his animal instincts to surface—whether by nature or through sheer will and strength of character.

Explanation:

This passage draws a stark contrast between raw human nature and cultivated refinement. The phrase "a man is generally an animal" acknowledges the primal instincts inherent in all humans—aggression, survival, and dominance. However, the true essence of a "gentleman" is defined by his ability to suppress these instincts, either due to an inherently calm disposition or through conscious self-discipline.

It also poses an implicit question: is gentleness a natural trait, or is it a learned behavior that requires effort and control? In a world where dominance and aggression are often celebrated, this passage serves as a quiet reminder that true strength lies in restraint.

www.ingramcontent.com/pod-product-compliance
Lightning Source LLC
Chambersburg PA
CBHW071714040426
42446CB00011B/2062